PRE

BY THE SAME AUTHOR

Television and its Audience
(Patrick Barwise and Andrew Ehrenberg)

Strategic Decisions
(edited by Vassilis Papadakis
and Patrick Barwise)

Media

**PATRICK BARWISE
and KATHY HAMMOND**

PHŒNIX

A PHOENIX PAPERBACK

First published in Great Britain in 1998 by
Phoenix, a division of the Orion Publishing Group Ltd
Orion House
5 Upper Saint Martin's Lane
London, WC2H 9EA

© 1998 Patrick Barwise and Kathy Hammond
The moral right of Patrick Barwise and Kathy Hammond to be identified as the
authors of this work has been asserted in accordance with the Copyright, Designs
and Patents Act of 1988

All rights reserved. No part of this publication may be reproduced,
stored in a retrieval system, or transmitted in any form or by any means,
electronic, mechanical, photocopying, recording, or otherwise, without the prior
permission of both the copyright owner and the above publisher of this book.

A CIP catalogue record for this book is available
from the British Library.

ISBN 0 297 81988 7

Typeset by SetSystems Ltd, Saffron Walden
Set in 9/13.5 Stone Serif
Printed in Great Britain by
Clays Ltd, St Ives plc

Contents

The digital revolution 1

The Jacksons in 2010 8

Relaxing 23

Staying in touch with friends and family 32

'A shopper's heaven'? 37

Work, education and healthcare 41

A better life? 45

And finally 53

Further Reading 54

The digital revolution

In 1840, midday local time in Bristol was ten minutes later than in London, 105 miles to the east. The mail coach took twenty hours to do the journey, so the time difference was of little concern except to sailors (who needed accurate time measurement to know how far east or west they were of the Greenwich meridian). The normal way to send an urgent message was by horse – just as it had been for the ancient Romans (who had better roads but smaller horses) and would still be for the US Pony Express twenty years later.

By 1856, the Great Western Railway and the electric telegraph had reduced the journey time to three hours and the communication time to a few seconds, and put Bristol and the rest of Britain on the same time as London. These two technologies dramatically reduced the effects of time and distance in Europe, and even more in large countries like the United States. A third technology, the steamship, accelerated emigration by poor Europeans to America and elsewhere, and helped European states to maintain global empires.

Twentieth-century communication technologies – telephones, cars, planes, radio, television – have increasingly shaped everyday life, now even in the poorest countries. Where, how and with whom we live and work, what we buy and where, how we relax, what we know, think and feel, have been determined as much by these media as by any other technologies, and this process has been almost continuous for at least 150 years.

Yet suddenly, since the mid-1990s, communication technology and its potential impact on everyday life have become hot topics. It is widely argued that we face a period of change even more dramatic, wider ranging and faster than any we have previously experienced. On this view we are in the early stages of a revolution comparable in scale to the biggest changes ever experienced by humans – the development of language, the change from hunter-gathering to farming, or from farming to industrial production. But today's revolution is happening much faster. According to some, within a generation – that is, by the time our children reach the age that we are today – everyday life will have changed completely.

This revolution and the society it heralds have been variously described: the 'information age', 'cyber-society', the 'third wave'. Here we use the term *digital revolution* to draw attention to its defining characteristic: the conversion of every kind of information into digital data.

Going digital

Traditionally, messages were copied, stored and transmitted using *analogue* technology. For instance, a telephone converted the sound waves of the speaker's voice into an electrical signal with a waveform as close as possible to that of the original sound. This signal was transmitted down the line to the receiver, where it would be converted back to sound waves. During transmission, the signal would become distorted and attenuated and pick up other noise. Because of high cost and low capacity, long-distance calls were expensive as well as poor in quality. Recorded music also used analogue media – a variable groove on a disc or a magnetic signal on tape. Radio, TV and mobile phones used electromagnetic analogue signals over the air. Cable and satellite TV, VCRs and even – until 1991 – the proposed high-definition television (HDTV) were all analogue technologies.

All these and other media are now converting to *digital* technology. For instance, on a modern phone network the sound of the speaker's voice (essentially, its loudness at different frequency bands) is sampled many times per second and converted into electronic pulses or 'bits'. A bit (short for BInary digiT) is the smallest unit of digital information, corresponding to some part of a storage or transmission medium which can be in one of two states like a light being either off or on, usually represented by 0 and 1. Replacing analogue with digital media brings several advantages.

Reproduction quality
Unlike a phonograph, which reproduces every scratch and distortion in the analogue recording, a digital system like a CD player merely has to decide which bits are zeros and which bits are ones. Digital media also encode extra bits which help error checking and correction. The original recording can thus be exactly reproduced.

More efficient channel use
With analogue technology, if you make a three-minute call from London to New York you tie up one of the lines on that route for the whole three minutes – no one else can use it at the same time. With digital telephony, several calls can share the same line without even being aware of it.

A common language
Unlike analogue technologies, which represent information in ways that reflect specific physical media (electric waves on a wire for telephony, radio waves for broadcasting), digital technology uses the universal language of bits. Any channel which can transmit or store bits can do so regardless of the content. So, subject to capacity, the same channel can be used for transmitting any combination of video, still pictures, audio/voice, text and data. For example, using the same channel you could contact a theatre, view a video clip of the play, check performance times, seats and prices (including what the stage looks like from each seat), select the day, time and seats that you want, have your credit card details verified, and print your own theatre tickets – although printed tickets will gradually disappear as the world becomes more electronic. All these different types of information can be transmitted as

packets of bits, with each packet having additional 'header' information to ensure that it reaches the right destination and that the receiving equipment knows what to do with it (for example, convert it back to audio or video).

The common language of bits also makes it possible to produce *multimedia* products: for instance, a CD-Rom or Internet website can have any combination of text, sound, still pictures and – again subject to capacity – video.

Data processing

Bits have always been the language of computers. Using computer programs, digital data from communication media can be manipulated, compressed, combined with other digital data such as customer records and processed in almost any way we like.

Because bits are a common language and can be manipulated, people often refer to *convergence*, meaning that, since different media are increasingly using the same digital technology, the past distinctions between them are disappearing. This has huge implications not only for how we can use media, but also for the media industries themselves. In particular, three large industries that were previously separate – telephones, television and computing – are becoming a huge industry which directly accounts for perhaps 10 per cent of world economic activity, and strongly impacts every other industry.

Why now?

People have been heralding the information revolution in various guises for at least thirty years. In the 1960s we already had talk of a post-industrial economy dominated by 'knowledge workers'. High hopes were held for the ability of computers to take over both routine tasks and strategic decisions, bringing in an age of unprecedented leisure for everyone. Some of these predictions were vividly illustrated in the 1968 film *2001: A Space Odyssey*, which introduced us to HAL, the highly intelligent talking computer which stole the show. The Japanese and US governments both studied the concept of 'wired cities' using cable TV to deliver entertainment, information and educational services similar to those discussed today in the context of the digital revolution. On the basis of these hopes, the US government allowed the cable companies to set up local monopolies. In the event, these never delivered anything other than television – with the understandable justification that user trials found minimal consumer interest in any of the other services, including interactive TV.

What, then, is different this time?

First, computers have become more powerful, cheaper, smaller, easier to use (although they still have a long way to go on this front) and more widely distributed, especially within businesses and especially in the US. Many of us now have personal computers (PCs) at home and also interact with computer technology in many other guises – games machines, automatic teller machines (ATMs) and the fifty microcomputers in a typical modern car.

Second, the Internet. The Internet is a loose network of networks which enables PCs in most large organizations and many homes and small businesses (using a standard connection to a telephone line) to communicate with each other around the world at low cost. The Internet belongs to no one (although it uses telecommunication links which do) and has no central authority; it is really a set of 'communication protocols', more like a language than a physical network, which means that any computer, whatever its internal language, can communicate with any other. The Internet has existed for many years as an academic network, but took off as a mass application only in the mid-1990s. This was partly because of the invention of new software (the World Wide Web and 'browsers') which made it easier to find useful information and move between different sites.

The Internet exhibits a characteristic crucial for all successful communication networks: that their value to each member increases with the number of other members. The same happened with telephones and, more recently, fax machines: neither would be useful – except as a status symbol – if no one else had one. Once enough other people were on the Web, it became worth while for yet more people. In reality, despite all the talk of Websites, 'surfing' and cyber-commerce, the main way most people (including the authors) use the Internet today is for electronic mail (email) – typed messages and documents sent from one PC to another. The email population reached 'critical mass' in about 1995.

The extent and speed of the digital revolution

Futurologists have not been very precise about how, and how much, digital media will change our lives. Most comment has focused on the expectation that consumers will soon be able to use their TV or PC to shop, bank and order movies from their armchair. Some commentators envisage more dramatic changes to everyday life. Nicholas Negroponte, director of MIT's Media Lab, believes that a key development over the next five years will be the 'personalization' of the computer, with wearable devices such as a wrist-mounted TV, computer and telephone. Peter Cochrane, head of research at British Telecom, looks further ahead, asking us to 'Imagine a virtual-reality interface, with your visual cortex flooded by information from spectacle-mounted or contact lenses augmented by directional audio input, tactile gloves and prosthetic arms and fingers that will give you the sensation of touch, resistance and weight.'

Historically, enthusiasts for new technologies have usually been over-optimistic about the *speed* of change. Most new technologies take longer to be adopted by the general public than these enthusiasts expect, although there have been exceptions: once they had reached critical mass, VCRs and mobile phones took off faster than most experts predicted. Arguably, everyday life in the advanced economies changed more between the 1880s and the 1930s than in the last fifty years or, possibly, the next. Nevertheless, it is valid to talk about a digital 'revolution', since the extent of change is dramatic by any standards and digital technology is its biggest single driving force. Even if the enthusiasts overstate how quickly things will change, they may turn out to be right about the *scale* of that change.

At this stage, no one knows how the digital revolution will develop. Although the technology itself is now becoming somewhat more predictable, exactly how, and how fast, things change will depend not only on technical developments but also on the policies of key commercial and political players, especially in the US. Less predictable is how enthusiastically consumers will take to this technology on an everyday, mass-market scale – the focus of our own research at London Business School. Least predictable are the sociocultural and geopolitical responses: will the digital revolution lead to greater international understanding or bitter rivalry? Will it encourage materialism and erode religious belief, or lead to a religious backlash? Will it make people happier? Here we concentrate on the likely impact of digital technology on everyday life.

To illustrate this impact let us fast-forward to the year 2010 and see what a typical day looks like for the Jacksons – an upper-middle-class nuclear family in the US, who have enthusiastically adopted digital technology.

The Jacksons in 2010

Pete Jackson is a manager and his wife Marion Jackson is a lawyer. They have two children, Lisa (sixteen) and Tim (twelve). In 2010 the Jacksons have a fully cabled home with a network connection in every room. Interaction with the household communications system (H-COM, described in more detail on page 15 is via a personalized intelligent agent, which the family call 'Bob'. What sorts of things do the Jacksons do in their interactive digital home?

Watching any programme you want, when you want

Tim Jackson has finished his school work. Some friends come over and they decide to watch an old movie, *Lethal Weapon*. In the family room there is a large flat screen on one wall. Tim presses his palm against the bottom right corner of the screen. It displays a picture of the Mars space probe and a menu with 'Tim' written in the centre. Bob's voice says: 'Hello Tim.'

Tim: 'Hi, Bob. Movies, please: *Lethal Weapon*, to start now.'

Bob: 'Tim, *Lethal Weapon* is R-rated. I'm afraid you do not have permission to watch this film.'

Tim and his friends decide on another film.

Tim: 'Bob, movies, please: *Space 2000* or something.'

Bob: 'Tim, is your chosen film *2001: A Space Odyssey*?'

Tim: 'Yes, that's it, Bob, yes.'

Bob: 'Tim, this film has a parental guidance rating, it is a Classic Movie, cost 99 cents. Please confirm when you are ready to start.'

Tim is allowed to watch parental guidance films and he has more than 99 cents left to spend this month in his personal H-COM account (Bob knows all this already). He confirms his choice: 'OK, Bob.' As the movie starts, a visitor from today would be struck by the wide, bright, sharp picture and – even more – the superb sound quality.

Ten minutes into the film another friend arrives. Tim says, 'Bob, pause the film, please. Restart from the beginning.'

The Jacksons can also ask Bob for more recent releases – at a price of up to $10 – or for any programme shown in the last twenty-four hours on any of 300 channels. Major live sporting events like the annual American Football 'Superbowl' cost up to $25. Most of their viewing, however, consists of watching programmes as they are transmitted on one of six main networks showing a mix of programmes, or one of the dozen bigger specialist channels showing news, sport or movies. Excluding 'video on demand' (for movies and classic TV shows) and 'pay per view' (for live special events, mostly sport), the H-COM service costs $50 per month (prices in 1998 dollars).

Homework, music and chat

Tim's sister Lisa is in her bedroom doing a school assignment on Stalin's purges. She uses paper and pencil to plan it and scribble notes, and a couple of textbooks as her main sources. She wants some background music, so she presses her palm against the teleputer screen in her room. It displays her menu and Bob says, 'Hi, Lisa.' She asks for her favourite radio station and then asks Bob to turn the volume down. She then asks for material on Stalin's purges and after a few minutes finds a good summary from *Encyclopaedia Britannica* which she downloads and prints out for easier reading and note-taking. She is also able to draw on material assembled by her teacher on the school's website, including film footage, maps and photos. Finally, she writes her assignment using a mixture of dictation and the keyboard, and incorporating – with attribution – pictures and text from several sources. When the assignment is complete, she submits it by email.

Bored, she decides to watch some music videos. She chooses 'new releases, UK', tries a couple of ten-second samples, and picks an album she has not heard before. She decides to buy it outright (that is, download it) for $10.99 rather than pay 99 cents for one play. As she has no more credit in her personal H-COM account, she checks her bank balance. Lisa's bank details are automatically encrypted and relayed to the music store. Authorization and download of the music video takes about thirty seconds. During the wait there is an ad for an online sportswear company.

Sitting down with a coffee to enjoy the music, Lisa decides to call her best friend Amy. She just says, 'Bob, I'd like to call Amy' (no hand-held receiver needed). An hour later, the music has gone back to the first track and the two friends are still chatting.

Grocery shopping

It's Pete's turn to cook this weekend. He turns on the kitchen H-COM teleputer. This is older than the family room screen or the bedroom teleputers and the built-in microphone no longer works well. Pete uses the menu system to select 'shopping', then 'weekly grocery list'. The Jacksons have a home-shopping account with their local supermarket, since they are not within the catchment area of any of the specialist online grocery warehouses. Pete calls up the weekly list and scans through it, deleting a few items with a screen pen.

The beer he usually buys is unavailable, so he checks the suggested alternative. Bob then lists some relevant special offers. The store brand of laundry detergent is being offered as three packs for the price of two. Pete checks 'yes'. He's asked whether he wishes to cancel his usual detergent order. He checks 'yes' again. Pete then selects 'browse' and then 'fruit and vegetables'. He chooses two ripe avocados and some multivitamin tablets from the healthcare section.

The home-shopping option adds $5 to the grocery bill and the boxed goods can be collected from the store or delivered to any address within ten miles. Pete decides on home delivery this week. It costs an additional $5 if the groceries are delivered Monday to Thursday (8.30 a.m.–5.00 p.m.), $8 for Friday to

Sunday or between 5.00 p.m. and 11.00 p.m. any evening. Pete chooses Thursday morning, when the home help comes, so she will be around to receive the delivery and pack the food away. The total bill plus delivery will be charged to the Jacksons' H-COM account.

Apart from groceries and entertainment, the Jacksons also use the H-COM to buy books, holidays, insurance, electronic equipment and many other products and services. For large purchases like a house or a car, they use it as an information source and to compare prices, or even to make the deal after a visit or test-drive. Most of their home shopping is initiated by themselves, as in the grocery example, but some is in response to a commercial. Instead of calling a freephone number to ask for information or make a purchase, they can do so via any of their teleputers.

Daily news

It's Marion's day for going into the office. Unusually for a US lawyer, she goes by train. On the journey, she uses her notebook communicator, a lightweight, touch-sensitive screen which opens to A4 size. She uses it mostly for reading and note-taking (with a screen pen). Marion forgot to connect her notebook to the H-COM before she left home, so to get her latest messages and updated personal news service, she connects to Bob through the mobile network. She pays for the connection by authorising a credit card payment. She then selects 'news', and then 'daily personalized information'.

There are eight stories on trademarks, her area of work. She reads these first, writing screen notes on three articles. She then flicks through the general news, stopping to read an item on educational reforms in Japan: secondary-school education is one of her interests and she is a parent governor of Tim's school. She reads some more articles from her special-interest sections, selecting some for transfer to a personal information folder. She also has eleven email messages. Four are in her work folder – she'll look at those in the office. Two messages are thought by Bob to be 'junk mail' (she has asked him not to delete messages unless he is pretty sure); one from a company she previously bought some educational software from, the other from a financial services site she visited on the Net. Marion deletes these as soon as she reads the title. There is also a message from Tim's school about an open evening, two bills, an email from her mother, and one from the local council, with a questionnaire on a proposed car toll system. Marion just has time to read and answer her mail before the train reaches her station.

Chatting with 'virtual' friends

Lisa and Tim's grandmother, Dora, belongs to several chat groups and also contributes to a bulletin board and newsletter for skin-cancer sufferers. The skin-cancer awareness newsletter (SCAN) is emailed to her once a week. Dora does not have an II-COM but her cable TV has a set-top box with a card reader and an infrared keyboard, so she can shop online and (most important) send and receive email.

Dora logs on to the Net at least twice every day. First thing each morning she checks her email. She has many friends and relatives around the world and locally (but not near enough to visit very often). Much of the morning is taken up with reading email messages and checking bulletin boards. Today she has seven messages including a long one from her friend Lilien about a recent holiday in Italy, together with video stills of Lilien with her grandchildren. Another is from her neighbour saying he has lots of spare tomatoes from his garden and he'll be round with them at 3.00 p.m. – Dora will not open her front door unless she is expecting someone.

There is also a message from the local church about a special service for seniors next week; a reminder from the health centre to come along on Thursday for a skin-cancer check-up; and a note from her daughter Marion inviting her to come on a family picnic this Sunday. Dora's bills also come by email – an electricity bill and a bank statement today. Dora has difficulty seeing fine print, but with email she can have every message displayed in large type on her TV screen.

After reading and replying to her email she goes to the SCAN Website. Dora is going for a skin-cancer check soon; she will go to her local community health practice for this, but will be examined and questioned remotely by a specialist in Boston. Dora has not had this type of examination before, so she wants to see if SCAN has an information page on remote health consultations.

A working day for the manager

This morning Pete is working from home before he makes a trip to check out a potential new site for the company, two hours' drive away. One reason for working at home this morning is that Pete's medical check is due. He had a minor heart attack last year and now has regular checks. A watch monitor logs his pulse and blood pressure. Once a week he connects to his clinic to transmit this information. If there is any cause for concern a health worker can call him on his video phone and, if necessary, he can chat to his doctor or arrange a personal visit.

Pete's home office has a teleputer like those in the bedrooms and kitchen, but he also has a video phone. While waiting for the results from the medical monitor, Pete dictates three letters and the draft outline of a report. He looks at the completed letters on his screen and makes small changes to the layout and wording using screen pen and voice. Pete then asks Bob to send the letters to his work network, to mark them as business (they are then automatically reformatted in line with the company corporate identity) and to see that the firm's system sends them out (electronically) with Pete's official signature and this morning's date and time stamp. Pete also asks Bob to copy the draft report to the other members of a task force on which he is working, with a note saying 'Draft, comments please.' The medical monitor report comes back, 'Fine, no action needed.' Pete slots his wallet computer into his terminal and says, 'Bob, copy my work in-tray to the wallet computer please.' Pete puts the wallet computer back in his pocket and is ready to leave home.

Pete's car has a personalized locking and ignition system which as he touches the door recognizes the wallet PC; the car requires the presence of the wallet PC and Pete's hand on the door to open, making it very difficult for any unauthorized person to open or start the vehicle. The garage opens up for him, he drives out and the garage closes after him. He slots his wallet computer on to the dashboard and presses 'on'. Bob makes contact with the car's voice-activated onboard system.

> Pete says: 'Hi Bob, directions please to a new destination, the old E-Zee-Rite paper factory at Rock Hill West, zip 22334.'
>
> Bob: 'Pete, would you like those directions as a printout, screen display or ongoing voice direction?'
>
> Pete: 'Bob, ongoing. Oh hell, I've forgotten to set the security.'
>
> Bob: 'Pete, I'm sorry, I do not understand. Please repeat.'
>
> Pete: 'Bob, ongoing voice direction, to start now. Also please set the house alarm and turn the heat to low.'
>
> Bob: 'Pete, ongoing voice direction activated. Journey time estimated at one hour forty minutes. From La Forge make a left on to Main Street, then first right to join the Interstate towards Rock Hill.'
>
> Bob continues: 'I have set the house alarm. Do you want the house heating set to low or the oven set to low or the car heating set to low?'
>
> Pete: 'Bob, the house heating. Now please connect me to my work in-tray and read out my messages.'
>
> Bob: 'Pete, Message 1 is a voicemail plus document from Jane Maynard in LA. Message follows: "Hi Pete, it looks as though that European deal may be trickier than we'd assumed. I've got the figures here. Have a look at them and let me know what you think." Pete, a three-page document is included – do you want me to read it out?'
>
> Pete: 'Bob, no, just give me a 10 per cent summary.'

Having listened to the summary, Pete says, 'Bob, call up Jane Maynard, please – her work number.'

Pete talks to Jane, then goes back to his mail, answering some, filing or deleting others. Bob tells him when to turn off the Interstate and directs him to the factory. From there Pete makes several phone calls on his wallet computer. On the way home he dictates his report. The following morning he is back in the office. The first meeting of the day is a video conference with other regional managers, builders and planners, to discuss the purchase of the site. Everyone has the plans, financial statements and draft reports available in the lower half of their screens. One accountant joins in the conference from home (though nobody notices as his video image is backed by his virtual office logo).

What have we assumed in these scenarios?

All the technology in these scenarios already exists, at least in a basic form, and is likely to be fully commercialized by 2010.

The Jacksons have access to a global communication system which is brought into their home and runs through it using cables, with one or more connection points in each room just like the electricity or telephone system today. Most of the intelligence is on a powerful home computer which is boxed away somewhere, like an electricity meter. Around the house the various digital appliances are plugged into this H-COM network. There is a large, flat, wall-mounted screen in the family room – probably still called the 'TV'. There are smaller teleputers in bedrooms, studies and the kitchen. These are like a present-day PC, but the screen is flat, thin and touch-sensitive and the keyboard is optional and not linked by wires to the screen. The teleputers also have speakers and a microphone, and some have a scanner, smart card or pocket communicator slot, camera or printer.

The Jacksons will probably have no telephones as we know them; all the terminals support voice calls, while some support two-way video. There are also pocket communicators with touch-sensitive screens, which combine a mobile phone, hand-held computer, smart card and so on. Some of these pocket communicators are fairly large (that is, book size), while others may be wallet, earphone or watch versions. They are mostly used when the Jacksons are on the move – in the car or train, or just in the garden. Using the network while on the move is possible with satellite/wireless technology.

Talking to Bob

One striking development is that the main way the Jacksons communicate with the H-COM is by voice rather than keyboard and mouse. All screens are also touch-sensitive and can be written on with screen pens. Some of the appliances still have keyboards. These are partly for backup (the way some cars still had a starter handle in 1960) but their main use is for error correction in complex documents which are mainly produced by dictation. A few very techno-enthusiastic friends of the Jacksons use gaze direction instead of touching the screen: some camera-equipped computers can tell where you are looking on the screen – even quicker and easier than pointing.

The other striking feature of the way the Jacksons communicate with the H-COM is the extent to which they rely on Bob, their software agent. Bob is usually represented by a disembodied male voice talking standard American-English. But he can be given a face and can talk in a number of different voices. Some households – or individuals within households – might choose a female persona and say 'she'. Hardly anyone refers to their software agent as 'it'. (Research by Byron Reeves and Clifford Nass at Stanford University shows that people naturally treat computers in many ways as if they were other people.) In 2010, Bob still sounds somewhat artificial but is improving all the time, both because of advances in technology (new software releases distributed automatically online) and also because 'he' is able to learn from experience.

An important part of the technology is Bob's ability to perform automatic speech recognition. Most communication with computers will be by people whose voices they already know, the main exception being organizational systems dealing with the general public. It should be possible to talk to a computer which knows your voice at normal conversational speed using natural language with its normal slurring ('how to wreck a nice beach' = 'how to recognize speech') with few errors. As with email today, for many purposes we will not be too fussy about errors, provided that they cause no misunderstanding. If a particular message or document needs to be 100 per cent correct, the system will be able to tell us about any words it was unsure of or, if necessary, we can go through the document on-screen or on paper and use voice/screen pen/keyboard to make corrections.

Technically, Bob is primarily an interface. Most of the intelligence he uses is distributed across different applications and other people's and organizations' systems. With both speech recognition and production, the system will need to have some understanding relevant to the particular context. The software is likely to be 'modular' with one module for each main application. One of the modules will be in effect a menu and will need enough vocabulary and knowledge to be able to route you into the appropriate application module. For instance, you should be able to say 'I'd like to read my email' or just 'email' or 'messages'. Similarly 'TV' or 'television' or 'what's on TV?' would trigger the television module, and so on for making a telephone call, dictating a message, shopping, watching a movie or conducting an information search (for example, 'I'd like to find out about . . .' or 'I want to look up flights to Chicago').

The reason for this approach – application-specific modules – is that, after more than thirty years of research, the goal of *general* artificial intelligence is still a long way away. Computers lack common sense, meaning the widely shared knowledge that people take for granted. For instance, if I enter a building on the ground floor and go up two floors I do not expect still to be at ground level. It is not hard to program a computer to know this too, but it will not know unless you have programmed it to do so. Similarly it is obvious to a person that it is usually inappropriate in the office to jump up, punch the air and scream with delight when something goes well; at a football match it might be inappropriate not to do so. Again, it would be anomalous for a cat to talk in real life but quite normal in a fairy story. To interpret speech enough to turn it into text requires some understanding of the immediate context in terms of other words and perhaps some specialized knowledge (for example, for a medical or legal context), but not this kind of broader common sense.

The only practical way to achieve anything like this apparent intelligence – essential, for instance, to produce more human-sounding speech from the computer – is to develop a series of specialized modules with detailed local understanding. If you ask Bob a question or ask him to do something that does not map on to one of these areas he will probably not understand – but should, at least, tell you so. In other words, the system in 2010 will be a collection of specialist parts tailored for particular applications, but sharing a common interface (unless you choose to have different interfaces for different applications). Increasingly, the different subsystems will also communicate with one another, so that if you are using Bob to keep your diary he might automatically remind you to buy a plane ticket or ask if you would like him to find out about flight times and prices. The nearest equivalent today is a good personal assistant with full access to most of your personal information and who also knows a lot about your habits and preferences.

By 2010 computers should also have some rudimentary emotional intelligence – something they totally lack at present. Bob's voice and talking head should be able to communicate some feeling through facial expression and intonation but are unlikely to look and sound natural. Similarly, Bob may be able to pick up some emotional signals, probably from the speaker's tone of voice. (Other possible cues include facial expression, body language, pulse and so on.) By 2010, manufacturers with more powerful computers may be able to use this facility to improve the design of products and services by detecting users' emotions during trials – such as irritation or pleasure. Examples might be the human interface with a banking system or a multichannel TV system, or the design of a new car.

For some applications, you will experience 'virtual reality' (VR). VR refers to technology which can be used to convince your senses that you are somewhere else, for example walking through an imaginary castle or a molecule, or flying a jet fighter; VR was initially developed for military training, where it is still widely used. The key component of VR is a helmet which immediately and accurately detects head movement and displays the resulting change in your field of vision. The Jacksons have a basic VR system for games. There are more advanced ones in Lisa's and Tim's schools, which are used for teaching history, geography and science.

The Jacksons can use Bob to access a wide range of services – live TV (which still exists), movies and other archival video and records, games and gambling, home shopping and banking, electronic 'newspapers', radio stations (which also still exist), educational services, email, voice and video phone, links to school and work networks, companies and information on the Web, and so on. Long-distance connections are so cheap as to be almost costless. Voice telephony and most data transfer (including audio and some video) are also virtually free: you will pay mainly for access to a specific level of capacity on the network, with little or no charge for usage. Payment for other services (Tim's movie, the grocery bill, Marion's mobile network connection) can be added to the monthly H-COM account with the Jacksons' communication services provider (for example, a phone company) or paid with a smart card or bank account details, with verification through a password or thumb print, for instance. Such systems can also deal with small amounts of 'cash'. Communications are scrambled ('encrypted') for security and electronic money exchange is at least as secure as with a credit card today.

There is a personalized menu for each member of the household. The menu offered to Tim and Lisa excludes 'adults only' channels: gambling, pornographic videos and virtual-reality shows, and adult-only chat lines. These can be accessed only by an identified adult. The communication link is two-way and interactive – that is, Tim can choose a movie (from a predetermined set) and when to see it, with rewind, fast-forward and search facilities, while the system knows which household to bill.

The H-COM does not have to be turned on. It is on all the time – monitoring lighting, heating and home security, receiving email, and so on. Meter reading is also done electronically. However, some applications do need to be activated by a switch or just a voice command. The identity of each user is usually verified by their voice, hand or thumb print, or iris pattern.

Many digital goods are delivered 'down the line'. Much of the information that exists on paper today will be available online, such as newspapers, telephone directories, travel time-tables, price lists, personal records. Most video and audio has become pay-per-view or available for purchase online. Groceries and other physical goods can be ordered online – but still have to be collected or delivered to the home.

For some sections of society, many more things are delivered to the home than at present, partly because of increased home working, partly because of the growth in domestic help. Society has become more polarized, with more work and rewards for successful knowledge workers, fewer and less skilled service jobs for the rest.

Will it happen? Technology and the market

Whether and how the digital revolution happens depends mainly on two factors: the continuing development of digital technology and the response of the mass market to the new products and services this technology makes possible. Also important is regulation. In the US, which will continue to dominate, the general trend will be for the role of government to be limited mainly to ensuring or encouraging competition. Other, more interventionist governments may slow down the pace of development but seem unlikely to change things fundamentally. Similarly, the way in which both technologies and markets are developed – and how quickly – will depend on the strategies of particular firms, especially those with a strong share of one of the important markets such as, currently, Microsoft in software and Intel in microprocessors, or an alliance between several such strong players. However, provided that the regulators ensure fair competition, the pace of technology and market development should be sustained.

In terms of infrastructure, we do not expect a switched broadband cable 'superhighway' reaching into almost every home like today's electricity grid. More likely is a continually evolving mixture of satellite, optical fibre, coaxial cable, various local wireless technologies – and many of the existing, ordinary telephone lines, especially if data compression techniques continue to improve. There may also be competition from electricity suppliers and other utility companies to carry data into and out of the home.

The terminal devices in the scenarios – screens, teleputers, Marion's electronic notebook – are simply later generations of existing technologies. One change over the next ten years will be the replacement of bulky cathode-ray tubes (in televisions and desktop PCs) with lighter flat-screen displays of equal or better brightness and sharpness.

Overall, the evidence is that the technologies assumed in our scenarios will be available as consumer products affordable by people like the Jacksons by 2010, and in some cases much sooner. The big question – more important and, at this stage, more difficult – is whether people will adopt and use these technologies on a large scale. No one knows, but by focusing on the consumer needs that the technologies are supposed to meet and the benefits that they are supposed to provide, we can make some informed judgements about the way the market is likely to develop.

In the next two sections we look at the impact of digital technologies on how media are used in the home for relaxing (such as watching TV) and keeping in touch (mostly by phone). We then look at some activities which presently take place largely outside the home – shopping, work, education and healthcare – and consider if, and how much, the digital revolution will change these activities, especially by bringing them into the home.

Relaxing

People watch television, listen to the radio and read newspapers, books and magazines mainly to relax. Of course, this is not clearcut. The BBC's mission is to 'entertain, educate and inform', and a good documentary or wildlife programme can do all three at once, as can a feature article in a newspaper. People also use media for other purposes: to energize them in the morning, to provide a shared viewing experience with their family, to give them something to talk about at work, and to reinforce their self-image.

The 'digerati' foresee massive change, with new interactive media largely replacing traditional forms, leading to quite different patterns of consumption and a blurring of the distinctions between media. Specifically, they foresee an end to the passive mass audience in which large numbers of people are simultaneously consuming the same content, chosen, packaged and scheduled by a small number of producers and editors. Instead, we are told, media audiences will become individualized and active. You will watch, read and listen to whatever you want, whenever you want, so that your morning paper and your evening TV viewing – and any advertisements you allow them to include – will be tailored to your individual preferences. Mass media as we know them will disappear.

This is largely hype. It is true that by 2010 most of the necessary technology will both exist and be affordable by people like the Jacksons. Media content will be produced in digital form and much of it will include extra index or keyword information – to allow easy storage, retrieval, sorting and other processing – such as which countries, people and topics are covered by a news item. However, the fact that technology exists does not in itself mean that it will be widely adopted and used. Changes will be both slower and less dramatic than the digerati predict, for two reasons.

First, economics. Despite the use of new technology to cut production costs, high-quality content will always be expensive and may become even more so as global media companies compete for the top events and talent. Interactive content will be even more expensive. The scope for general extra revenue from subscriptions and advertising is limited, although transactions like Pete Jackson's grocery shopping will bring some new money into the system (diverted from traditional channels like shops and bank branches and the cost of driving to them).

Second, and even more important, is human psychology. At least in its more extreme forms, the revolutionary vision ignores the fact that most people, most of the time, relax by being passive. This is typified by television, which people around the world watch passively for an average of about three hours a day.

Historically, old media have tended to adapt and find new roles in response to the launch of successful new media. Thus, both radio and magazines are thriving in new roles which complement television. Newspapers are still very much alive and so is the cinema, albeit on a much smaller scale than before TV. We expect all the existing mass media to survive, although there will be some minor exceptions. (For instance, we expect chemical photography to disappear as a mass market, continuing mainly as a medium for artists and hobbyists, like calligraphy today.)

Television: from broadcasting to narrowcasting?

Digital television (by satellite or cable) allows literally hundreds of channels. Many people expect this to change fundamentally the nature of television programming and viewing, from a 'broadcast' medium (dominated by big networks like Britain's BBC and ITV and the big US networks, showing a mixture of programme types with something for everyone) to a 'narrowcast' medium more like today's magazines and radio. On this narrowcast model, each channel would specialize in a particular niche: one programme type aimed at one specific target market.

One widely assumed benefit of this approach is that, as with magazines, the audiences of these niche channels would be strongly segmented, so that, for instance, the gardening channel would be mostly watched by home owners with gardens, many of whom would be relatively affluent retired people. The argument is that, as with gardening magazines today, such a channel could generate revenue both from subscriptions (since it would be tailored to that target audience) and from advertising (not just for gardening products, but also for other products and services such as cruise holidays and financial services aimed at the same target market).

Some of this is happening already, especially in countries with high cable penetration, notably the USA where the average family already has fifty channels. However, even in homes with fifty channels, half the viewing is still of the four national terrestrial networks or of local, public or cable channels showing general mixed programming.

More important, even for the niche channels the degree of audience segmentation and involvement is surprisingly low. For instance, whereas US radio stations are typically listened to by relatively few people but for many hours per week, the niche TV channels are watched only occasionally by those who watch them at all. This reflects a fundamental difference between radio, which people mostly listen to as a secondary activity while working or driving, and television which – although watched fairly passively and often combined with desultory eating or conversation – is a primary activity. People listen to radio to take their minds off what they are doing. They watch television to take their minds off what they are not doing.

Of course, the audience for sport channels – especially some sport – does tend to be male and that for music videos tends to be young. These differences are reflected in the products and services advertised. But these audiences are not distinctive enough to persuade advertisers to pay more per viewer on these niche channels than on the big general programming networks. This is quite different from, say, national newspapers in Britain, where the advertising cost per 1,000 readers of the *Financial Times* is twelve times as much as for the massmarket *Sun* or *Mirror*.

What, then, will happen if we have 500 channels rather than 50? First, many of those channels will be used for 'near video on-demand' (NVoD), where a two-hour movie is shown continuously on, say, six channels with start times at twenty-minute intervals. On this basis, a choice of twenty movies would require 120 channels. This would reduce the market for video rentals and perhaps, at the margin, outright sales of video cassettes.

Second, channels with spare content will repackage it into several narrower offerings, such as a channel owned by a Hollywood studio showing only classic horror movies or westerns. This approach will give content owners and producers more options to generate viewers and a way to try and develop a distinctive positioning in an increasingly crowded market.

The main constraint is the scarcity of high-quality programming. Increasing the number of channels in itself has no more effect on the supply of programming than increasing the number of estate agents would have on the supply of houses. For the same reason, the scope for locally originated television (for example, from the local community) is quite limited: the local audience is too small to support high-quality programming. The best that can be realistically achieved is some viewing of local news and sport.

Putting the consumer in control
Simply increasing the number of TV channels, then, seems unlikely to change radically what and how people watch. Potentially more important is the ability of digital technology

to shift control from media producers to consumers. Increasingly, technology will allow us to ask for the information we want, whenever we want it. Initially this may be mainly through explicit selection by browsing a menu or conducting a search using keywords. Over time, you will be able to delegate more to a personal assistant like Bob.

This potential shift from a model where producers 'push' information out to the public to one where consumers 'pull' only what they want, when they want it, applies to all media including television. The networks will still, as now, broadcast a continuous schedule of programmes, with the most current (especially sport) and appealing shown at prime time to maximize the number of people who watch them as they are shown. But, well before 2010, you will be able, with little effort (and without having to remember to ask a teenager to set the VCR), to watch any programme from any channel, shown any time in the last week, or year, whenever you like and in any order. *You* will be in control.

It is hard to say how much this will actually happen. Our hunch is that, most of the time, people in 2010 will still switch between a few main networks and a few more specialized ones, watching the best (or the 'least worst') programmes on air at the time. As now, they will use habit, memory and familiar brands – particular channels, shows and artists – to simplify programme choice. Nevertheless, we expect the amount of time-shifted viewing to increase and at least some people to use their personal assistants to search out and filter much of what they watch. In Nicholas Negroponte's words, 'Today's TV set lets you control brightness, volume and channels. Tomorrow's will allow you to vary sex, violence and political leaning.' One result may be that you are less likely to see anything that questions your beliefs or values.

Interactive TV

Digital technology can also make the experience of watching a particular programme more interactive than now. So far, the most successful application of interactive TV has been to game shows. You, the viewer at home, can also have your finger on the buzzer and compete against the studio contestants – or against others in your own and other homes. With an online connection, this can be for prizes or for the chance to be a studio contestant next week. It costs little to add the required data to an existing game show and increases the audience's involvement and enjoyment. Once enough homes are online, new game shows will be designed specifically to exploit this technology.

Another application is to overlay a programme with further background information. Examples include detailed team news and statistics for sports enthusiasts (especially suitable for sports like American football where the action is discontinuous), recipes on food shows and booking information on holiday programmes. The ability to 'find out more' is one of the hallmarks of digital technology.

With sports, the technology can also let you select camera angles, look at action replays, pit your wits against the coach by calling the next play, join in fantasy football, or (subject to regulation) place a real bet on who will win. Sport generates high viewer involvement, so several of these applications may be viable, although some – such as choosing camera angles – may increase production costs too much.

There have also been many experiments with interactive fiction or drama in which your own actions affect the plot – deliberately or otherwise. This is true of fantasy games, although these happen in real time using the present tense ('you are in a room with three doors...') rather than telling a story about something which has supposedly happened in the past ('it was a dark and stormy night...'). Generally, narrative fiction – novels and movies – will stay linear and always aim for involving characters and a strong plot with a beginning, a middle and an end. And, on the whole, consumers will prefer to continue delegating the storyline to Shakespeare or Jackie Collins.

Interactive TV will enhance many viewers' enjoyment of game shows, sport and magazine-type programmes. However, it will not turn television into something quite different, partly because some of the more radical options would be too expensive to programme routinely, partly because even in 2010 people will not want to read large amounts of text on a TV screen, and partly because interaction usually requires more effort than most viewers want to make most of the time.

The evidence, then, is that TV viewing will not be so very different in 2010 compared with now. The total amount of viewing may decline, especially for younger people, as the number of competing activities increases. We will also have to pay directly for more services – that is, there will be relatively more pay-per-view and subscriptions and perhaps less advertising-funded TV. There will be somewhat more timeshift viewing, more fragmentation of the audience because of the increasing number of channels, probably even more channel switching and 'grazing' than today, and rather more lone viewing, partly because of the increasing number of screens per home, but also because the number of one-person households will increase.

None of these trends is new. Remote switches, multiset homes, video games and VCRs have been with us for many years – and yet what and how people watch is not different in kind from thirty years ago. Major live events – the Olympic Games, the arrest and trial of O. J. Simpson or the funeral of Diana, Princess of Wales – provide a widely shared experience. Live events and top-rated movies and TV shows will continue to do so. In fact, with a global audience and multiple screening opportunities, the most popular aspects of mass culture will be even more widely shared than today. We also expect much TV viewing – more than half of evening viewing, except in single-person households – still to be done in company. People will still want to flop down in front of the television in 2010 much as they do today. In an increasingly complex and stressful world, the need for relaxing, passive entertainment – epitomized by TV – will be greater than ever.

Turning to other entertainment media, high-definition TV and video on-demand will not kill off the cinema. We like to go out in company and there will always be technologies which are too expensive to bring into the home. Some cinemas in 2010 may allow us to experience state-of-the-art virtual reality or holographic imagery. Computer games – mainly played by boys and young men – have boosted the acquisition of powerful home PCs. Multiplayer games can also lead to experimentation with other online relationships (for example, electronic 'bulletin boards' to exchange ideas or products). Games are now poised to become one of the main uses of virtual-reality technology, although this is likely to occupy only a small corner of the overall interactive media market.

Gambling will probably be a larger industry than games. It is already larger, in terms of annual revenues. In many countries gambling is state regulated and taxed, and offshore online gambling can evade these controls. The opportunity for gambling on live broadcast events, and the immediacy of the (possible) rewards, also make online gambling an exciting prospect. We are more sanguine about the possible increase in pornography. Concerns over pornography have dominated the early years of the Internet, as with most media when new, from books to videos. Sites with an overtly sexual nature will continue to grow on the Internet, but they will make up a small and ever-decreasing percentage of total content and usage. As Internet guru Esther Dyson suggests, a combination of rating and filtering services will emerge which will make it easier for families to control which information comes into the home.

Print media

The main current barrier to the general adoption of online newspapers is the lack of a small, light, cheap, robust storage device with a bright, sharp, page-sized viewing screen. As batteries get smaller and longer-lasting, and screens become easier on the eye and touch-sensitive (so keyboards are no longer needed), we will see more computers being read on the move. Even so, it is unlikely that many people will switch to simple electronic versions of today's newspapers. This is partly because printed newspapers cost so little and partly because, even in 2010, electronic newspapers will still be expensive to provide to people on the move.

The main attraction of an online newspaper is that it can be customized and is interactive. Customization means that you can choose what sorts of stories to see. You might select all the major news items, plus anything on New Zealand, all items on children's education, no fashion stories, no sports, and the weather/traffic and news for your local area. Again you may wish to see no advertising, or only specific types of ads, or you may subscribe (free) to various advertising-only services. You could also choose from a variety of editorial styles – perhaps a different style and content for Saturday and Sunday compared with the weekday/workday format. It would be hard to get the mix right first time, so you would continue to adapt and personalize it over time.

Digital newspapers have another advantage over print-on-paper: they can contain audio and video clips as well as print. Also, the advantage of interactivity means that you can point (or click or touch with a light pen) and request more information on a topic, or send an electronic message to the author or editor, or respond to ads, or race to be the first to finish the crossword. As described in the Marion Jackson scenario, portable notebooks or 'tablets' can also be used for sending and receiving both real-time (phone) and delayed (email, voicemail) messages. Turning to books, non-fiction and – especially – reference books will adapt well to going online, but books, particularly fiction, will not disappear.

Staying in touch with friends and family

Apart from relaxing, the other main use of media in the home is to keep in contact with people we like or love. Most residential telephone use today is social and local. We expect this to continue in the future. In 2010, there will be three interpersonal digital media – email, voice phone and video phone – although the distinctions between these will blur.

Email

Email is the great recent success story of digital technology. It is simple, cheap and meets real needs. Although all the hype about the Internet focuses on sophisticated applications like complex information searches or home shopping, most of the actual use of it is for email. Much current growth is among the retired: email is a wonderful medium for keeping in touch with people around the world at low cost, with little effort and with minimal delay from the time a message is sent to the time the recipient can read it. Unlike the phone (unless you have switched to voicemail), email is non-intrusive: you look at your messages when it suits you. This makes it especially well suited for communication between very different time zones.

Email is also flexible. For people who know each other well, most email messages are short and informal, without much fuss about usage or spelling – more like a casual spoken conversation than a written document. At the same time, email can also be used more formally – an email contract can be legally binding – or to transmit a large document. Again, an email can easily – perhaps too easily – be copied to large numbers of people with minimal extra effort. It can be as complex and elaborate as any other document: Bill Gates,

Chairman of Microsoft, likes to handcraft birthday cards for his close family using recent digital snapshots.

As with the telephone today, not everyone will have email at home in 2010, even in the most advanced economies. This problem can be reduced by recycling terminals, by the market supplying some very cheap and simple ones (probably combined with a voice phone) and by providing access in community centres and other public spaces. In addition, governments may allocate a 'default' email address to every citizen.

One development of email is the growth of 'virtual communities' sharing a common interest such as Corgi toy cars or the genealogy of Clan Maclean. Electronic media are ideal both for identifying people with similar interests and for servicing the shared needs and tastes which come about from hobbies, lifestyle or illness. For some people, such virtual communities will be the 'killer application' that grabs and keeps their interest in the information network.

Voice phone

We also expect continuing growth in voice telephony, especially long-distance and mobile telephony. By 2010, when the normal input device will be a hidden microphone rather than a keyboard, the distinction between email and voice phone will be less clearcut than today – a question of which form of output the receiver chooses (assuming their system has up-to-date voice processing). For simultaneous dialogue, people will usually choose voice, as now. This will normally be the unprocessed voice of the speaker, with perfect clarity and no perceptible time lag even for a conversation halfway round the world. By 2010, the H-COM should also be able to translate between languages in real time, although both the translation and the synthesized voice will be less than perfect, especially if the system does not know both speakers.

Increasingly, however, we will be leaving each other messages. For a short message, you will just leave a recording of your voice, like voicemail today. For any longer or more complex message, you will tell the system to leave an email and it will automatically convert what you say into digital text. In 2010, the coding will still be less than perfect, but the sender will be able to make corrections on her own screen if the detail of the message is important.

The main difference in 2010 is that telephony will be mostly 'hands off' – as in Lisa's conversation with her friend Amy. Calling someone should be easier than now. For close family and friends, you will be able to say just 'Call Janet' or 'Get me Janet'. (If that sounds too abrupt, the personal assistant can easily be instructed not to respond unless you also say 'please'.) Most phones are likely to be portable and pocket-sized. Telephones today are actually harder to use than in the past, because they have so many features. By 2010, they should have become simple again, since all the features will be managed by software with little effort by the user.

Video phone

What is less clear is the extent to which we will have two-way video capability. Leaving aside the technology and the costs – these will already be less of a barrier by 2010 – the main objection to video telephony is that few of us want to be seen at home by strangers, even if we ourselves can see the other person on our screen. In one of the early Japanese trials of interactive TV with two-way video, families put on their best clothes and specially cleaned their – doubtless already spotless – homes before each evening's transmission.

This problem is easily solved. If you do not want callers to see you, you can simply turn off the two-way video link, or substitute a picture of yourself, your family or anything else. We believe close friends and family may over time prefer to see each other as they speak. The growing use of video conferencing at home by professionals, like Pete Jackson, will make people increasingly comfortable with this technology. The trick will be to make it more like a face-to-face conversation, for instance by ensuring that the image of the other person is at a comfortable distance and that the speakers maintain sufficient eye contact without staring at each other in an unnatural way. Assuming this happens, we expect most domestic video telephony to be among people who know each other well and talk often, mostly women and teenagers. We also expect most of the use to be local, as with the telephone today. This assumes that by 2010 families like the Jacksons are paying for a link to the network with enough capacity to support two-way video telephony and that most of the cost is for access rather than usage.

One consequence of what the *Economist*'s Frances Cairncross calls 'the death of distance' is that by 2010 it should cost little more to conduct a video conversation over any distance than it does to conduct a voice conversation today. The only exceptions will be where the person at the other end is somewhere very isolated or with underdeveloped infrastructure.

Firms may take a lead by adopting a video telephone number for their customer service department. This is likely to happen first in a business-to-business context and then in organizations dealing directly with the public. Our hunch is that most firms will prefer to show the service representative in person (rather than a computerised talking head), which will seem more human, natural and sincere. A possible scenario is a customer service representative who can be seen by, but cannot see, the consumer (this will, however, be quite stressful and difficult for the service representative, who will require training and support). The consumer may then choose to reveal her real face too, although this will mean sitting down in front of a camera-equipped terminal – something that one-way video telephony would not require.

However, people may still prefer voice-only telephony in 2010, even with their closest friends. Research suggests that people talk more freely, deeply and intimately on the phone than face to face. Even if video telephony does take off, most telephone conversations are likely to be voice-only in 2010, especially those conducted on the move.

One issue in the information society will be for people to keep control of the mass of incoming communications including unwanted phone calls and junk email. By 2010, a personal assistant like Bob will be able to put you largely back in control. Bob will know who you are happy to receive messages from at all, and with what priority (for example, live phone, voicemail, email), and will be able to sort and categorize recorded messages and, increasingly, summarize them too: just like a good personal assistant, and improving all the time with experience and feedback.

'A shopper's heaven'?

Bill Gates's view is that:

> All the goods for sale in the world will be available for you to examine, compare and, often, customize. When you want to buy something you'll be able to tell the computer to find it for you at the best price offered by any acceptable source. Servers distributed world-wide will accept bids, resolve offers into completed transactions, control authentication and security, and handle all other aspects of the marketplace, including the transfer of funds ... It will be a shopper's heaven.

Gates also suggests that we will examine product reviews online, check out relevant regulatory data and email people we know for recommendations.

Well, maybe, for some people and for some types of product. While online shopping will grow, there are several problems. Buying computer software online is straightforward and reliable. Buying peaches, crockery or a dress is not, because of the problem of physical delivery and the difficulty of judging colour, texture and quality from the screen.

Information will probably eventually be digitized for almost all products and services. But because it has to be made available to home online systems, different H-COMs must be on networks which are linked and can communicate with each other. Even more problematic, your intelligent agent ('Bob') must have access to all relevant information. For instance the system of which your H-COM is part might have exclusive rights to display Armani clothes or Sainsbury groceries, while another system might have exclusive rights to show Nike sportswear or Paramount movies.

Most fundamental of all, most people enjoy real-life shopping and browsing, at least for some products and services, some of the time. Bob will not have opinions on what suits you, nor will he be able to make small talk about last night's football match or the proposed city centre by-pass. Much shopping has a social side, especially for those who telework: home-based teleworkers are among the least enthusiastic groups when it comes to using their PCs for shopping and other non-work activities.

Electronic payment and banking

Telephone banking has been one of the success stories of the 1990s. This trend to remote banking will continue with screen-based services taking over from purely telephone-based services as more consumers go online. Successful online banks will be those who back up their system with helpful service staff. If you are reading your monthly statement on the screen and have a query, you will simply press or click an on-screen button which connects you by voice to a bank employee (perhaps working from their home) whose screen displays the same information as yours.

We will also see fewer cash transactions. Electronic cash or credit will become more widely used. One bonus is that this will simplify shopping abroad. Most of us are not too worried about giving our name, address and credit card number to a mail-order company or ticket agent over the telephone. Increasingly we will give this information via a screen-based display rather than by phone. Initially, screen-based transactions will involve menus and a little typing. Soon you will be able to speak your instructions (within a fixed format) and see them appear on the screen. Other forms of electronic payment, such as subscription accounts and digital money (held in the form of an electronic smart card) will also become widespread.

Professional services

For some kinds of people and for some sorts of advice, video consulting will provide many benefits. Video-consultations will probably involve the client and the professional each sitting in front of a screen, perhaps the same screen used for entertainment or work in the home. So if your time is valuable (and your income high) you may choose video consultation with your doctor, lawyer or interior designer.

It has been suggested that for the time-poor, especially those whose diaries are managed by others, software will be available to schedule meetings electronically. This may work for business colleagues who know each other well, or if you wish to meet with a lawyer, dentist or government official, where there are fixed booking rules. It will work less well for other professionals or for social appointments, which usually involve some polite negotiation.

Electronic information and advertising

If a TV commercial catches your attention, one or two clicks on your remote will get you more information straight away. You can view this information then or later and even order the product online. But often consumers want information about more than one manufacturer. An online information system may make it easier to obtain independent advice – for example, from consumer organizations or regulatory bodies. This online advice will especially appeal to the sorts of people who currently subscribe to *Which?* or *Consumer Reports*. The traditional bundling together of advice and sales may become less prevalent. More likely, markets will segment, as we are starting to see with people buying PCs: experienced PC users buy online while first-time buyers who need advice go to specialist retailers and pay a bit more for an equivalent machine.

As more of our TV viewing is elective (pay-per-view, video-on-demand), we may choose not to see as much general advertising as now. The trend towards more subtle advertising may continue – commercials that entertain, games and competitions, sponsorship. Classified ads will also naturally migrate to new searchable media. Elective viewing of advertising will help keep down channel subscription costs. You might also charge the company for this information – although how much you can charge will depend on how desirable you are as a potential customer.

The trend towards targeting and 'one-to-one' (that is, individual) marketing will continue, increasingly based on companies' records of people's individual characteristics and especially their previous transactions. For instance, you and your neighbour may both watch the same programme but see different commercials because one of you owns a cat (and buys cat food) and the other is a frequent business-class flyer. This raises privacy issues as well as other practical problems.

Work, education and healthcare

Apart from shopping, the new media will also allow you to do other things at home which now (since the industrial revolution) happen elsewhere.

Home versus office

As more people work from home, at least for some of the time, the line between work-time and home-time is becoming less clearcut. As industries become automated, more of the workforce is engaged in storing, processing and disseminating information, often using a telephone and a networked computer. Also, it is now easy and cheap (and becoming cheaper) to route information to and from any location. Virtual networks have developed where bank enquiries can be answered from operators sited anywhere, even abroad. A bank might have groups of remote enquiry handlers in a number of third-world countries, to benefit from both cheaper wages and time-zone differences.

Those who choose to 'telework' have tended to be the most autonomous workers: lawyers, accountants, academics or salespeople, who spend a growing – although still small – proportion of their work time at home in a room equipped with a networked PC/fax/printer and phone. These are not people who 'clock on' and work a set number of hours a week. Rather they are judged by results, and their jobs have always involved taking some work home. For such workers, offices might eventually become places you visit one or two days a week to share experiences with colleagues and have meetings. Digital technology will not greatly reduce travel by professionals: it can substitute for some journeys but also makes travel time more productive. Wherever you go, your virtual office can go with you.

The other group of people for whom telework is increasing may not welcome the change. These are workers whose job entails sitting in front of a PC wearing a phone headset: for example customer support staff can have access at home to both customer and company records. Such changes in workplace practices are primarily being driven by large corporations looking for savings in wages, office space and overheads. While the chance to work for a large bank from your cottage in the country may seem attractive, there are costs as well.

It has been suggested that telework is ideal for those with small children: the parent works in one room while children play in the next. If the baby wakes up and needs feeding, the mother can signal that she is unavailable for work until all is quiet again. This could approach the grim type of life experienced by out-workers in the clothing trade (the PC taking on the role of sewing machine, with payment based on the number of enquiries handled). It could represent a backward shift in employee conditions: no office or canteen socialization, less chance of training, promotion or even 'sick-pay'.

Both these types of telework will increase over the next twenty years, although much less than most of the digerati suggest: even in California, the actual incidence of telework from home using networked PCs is less than 1 per cent of total working days.

Education

Successfully exploiting computers in schools has proved to be a desperately slow process over the last twenty years, but the pace of change will accelerate over the next ten. Many changes will be incremental. As schools join the information network they will probably have access to a special school network and database where information has already been coded, vetted and sorted, and where children can chat online to other children around the world. Encyclopaedias are better online and computers are good at taking children in a measured and non-judgemental way through any learning which is based on facts and rules. However, establishing and maintaining such a project will require substantial government investment, especially if it is to help those most in need, children who are not linked to the network at home. Without strong government intervention, electronic media will do little to equalize children's education. Some schools will have a state-of-the-art personal notebook computer for every child, others will have one older PC for every class.

Even with appropriate investment and teacher training, electronic media will play only a small part in school life in 2010. School is still about socialization and about learning things which cannot be digitized: the making and breaking of friendships, the meeting and melding – often more than at any other time in a person's life – of people from different backgrounds, cultures and physical and mental abilities.

Healthcare

Medicine is also benefiting from innovations brought about by the adoption of digital media. Patient records – doctors' notes, X-ray images, pathology slides, videos of speech impairment or behavioural problems – are starting to be routinely stored electronically and accessed remotely by different healthcare agencies. In the last few years we have also seen time-savings in the treatment of patients at small rural hospitals, where high-speed data links have connected local sensors, ultrasound scans or X-ray equipment to specialist doctors and diagnostic centres.

The most dramatic change (especially for the patient) is the ability for blood pressure, heart beat, body temperature and so on to be monitored remotely. This telemedicine saves time and money for healthcare providers and reduces travel and stress for patients in remote communities. With networked health centres and then individual networked homes, many more basic medical practices will take place remotely. Eventually, face-to-face contact with your doctor may be the province of the rich, the poor and the really sick.

Another trend in medicine is that people are increasingly seeking to become more knowledgeable about the workings of their own bodies. This is seen in self-diagnosis and patient (especially patient-to-patient) support. Computer-based patient support systems give users medical information – but at the user's own pace and preserving the user's anonymity. Patient-to-patient support is ideally suited to digital media. Some medical problems are like obsessive hobbies which can consume your every waking moment. What you need is fellow sufferers, who may not live near by. A global network such as the Internet is ideally suited for sharing and disseminating specialist medical information and experience – a good example of a virtual community.

A better life?

Some commentators predict a digital utopia: greater equality in education; more control over our lives; less pressure on natural resources (because more products will be in the form of bits rather than manufactured goods); politicians becoming more sensitive to public opinion; increased understanding, tolerance and global peace (due to increasing economic interdependence and more open communication); even improved writing and reading skills (as young people use email).

The most optimistic envisage a global communication network potentially linking every home with every other home and with all stored digital information. This will give us the ability to receive/send words, pictures and sounds from/to any other person or institution connected to the network. We will even be able to do all of these things while we are on the move. However, the ability to send and receive information, even if we can do it faster and more easily than ever before, does not necessarily mean that there will be more *communication* – or understanding. Below we consider other potential advantages and disadvantages for society in general.

The digital revolution will probably displace more jobs and create fewer new ones than earlier social revolutions. The fear of unemployment, automation or smart systems making your job redundant means that those who have work will work harder. As Frances Cairncross of the *Economist* writes,

> The fragmentation of the large employer has made many workers feel less secure. More and more people employed on short term contracts, or as freelancers, will be only as good as their last job and under constant pressure to find the next assignment before the current one finishes. The blending of

leisure and work may well mean in practice that work increasingly intrudes into leisure: it makes for more forceful demands.

A knock-on effect of less commuting (plus improved traffic management) would be fewer traffic jams, especially during rush hours. In reality, there is unlikely to be less traffic, but traffic will become more managed. Road pricing (electronic tolls), automatic speed traps (remote sensing of car registration) and smarter cars (that talk to you and, eventually, drive themselves, at least on main roads) will become widespread. Using low orbit satellites and radio sensors, vehicles can be tracked as they travel, enabling companies to fine-tune delivery schedules, or monitor expensive or dangerous equipment.

Digital video cameras, online networks and global positioning systems will be used to monitor employees, company equipment including vehicles, personal equipment (homes, cars or boats) and even family members (the young and the old or ill). Employees who might find themselves monitored by video include teleworkers and public employees potentially subject to abuse or claims of abusive behaviour (social workers, doctors, nurses, police).

Remote tracking is an example of a 'new' application rather than just a faster or cheaper way of doing an existing task and will find many more applications. For example, prisoners can be electronically tagged, or people with certain medical complaints can live at home on their own with a discreet monitor which sends a message to their doctor or hospital if they are in danger.

One widespread fear is that digital technology will lead to reduced human contact. This seems unlikely. As illustrated by the Jacksons, people with the technology, including the elderly living alone, will actually use it to increase their contact with others outside the home. Within multiperson households, however, communication between family members will continue to be reduced.

Inequality

All technologies tend to disadvantage those who do not have access to them. If you do not have a car, large out-of-town supermarkets are largely inaccessible, you miss out on lower prices and your local shop may close down through lack of business. On balance, the digital revolution will widen inequality in society. Once homes have paid to be linked to the information network, much of the information available to them will be free or cheap. Transmission charges will also be low.

Those not connected to the network may have to pay more than at present to receive information in paper form (for example, telephone directories, encyclopaedias, local newspapers). As electronic mail becomes widespread, postal charges may rise. With the increase in the take-up of satellite and cable television, the service available on UK broadcast TV is already narrowing: many sports events, previously broadcast free, can now be seen only on pay-TV. This trend will accelerate unless the BBC licence fee is allowed to increase more in line with the costs of world class programming.

Crime and security

City centres, car parks, playgrounds, homes, offices, factories and roads will all become equipped with video cameras. But although crimes will be more easily monitored, criminals will not necessarily be more easily identified. It is true that you can search digital video looking for a particular face – but that face then needs to be matched to a known existing one. Even if we all have compulsory identity cards with our picture and a full record of our visual characteristics, and this information is stored on a police network, it will be hard to match this information with video footage. For the foreseeable future humans will remain better equipped than computers to remember and recognize faces, especially at unusual angles and displaying unusual expressions. People in third-world economies may be employed to watch the security monitors.

Monitoring children in the playground or at the nursery may safeguard against kidnappers and abusers. But how many parents would be happy accompanying their child to the playground knowing that their every word and movement was being captured on video? The video camera can protect, but also frighten. Video images can easily be altered – the face of your child playing on the swing superimposed upon less innocent images. The power can also be switched off, the video camera covered or tricked into recording a picture which is not current. So video cameras are not a foolproof way of making the environment safer.

Data protection is more difficult with an electronic and interactive medium. Even the most secure encryption system is vulnerable to illicit access to the password. Those who have committed crimes on the Internet have tended to come from the same community as the developers; crime innovates at the same rate as anything else. So we will have theft and espionage and infringement of copyright and libel and child pornography in this new medium. Apart from the privacy issues, there will probably be few new crimes: just familiar crimes in new guises.

How will we prove that a crime has taken place? Paper records, audio and video tapes and photographs used to be taken as hard evidence, as facts. In the future, if we do not agree with the evidence, we will assume that it has been digitally altered. Criminals will exploit this. One solution is for digital images to be 'stamped' with a time, date and electronic 'watermark', but this may be insufficient to provide the certainty we are accustomed to from physical evidence.

There are other dangers. Because of competitive pressure, companies are launching services based on cutting-edge, rather than tried and tested, technology. Software and networks are increasingly complex and interconnected. The whole system may have unpredicted weaknesses and vulnerabilities, exemplified by the 'millenium bug'. When information is available *only* online, what happens if the central server on which information is held breaks down or becomes corrupted by cyber-terrorists? What happens if an electronic 'Pearl Harbor' is launched by a hostile state? These are real risks, ignored by most techno-enthusiasts.

Privacy

Traditionally, your bank was the only commercial service that knew what you earned, how you earned it and (to some extent) what you spent it on. Various government agencies also recorded demographic details and noted which cars you had owned, where you had lived and if you had a criminal record. Now, an increasing number of private companies and agencies gather and store information about you, much of which you cannot easily check. This is held on networked computers and used for purposes that you might not like (if you knew). By 2010, Bob and other agents and systems on the network will hold all manner of information on the Jacksons' likes, dislikes and private habits.

Much of this information will be on your home information system, which is connected to the global information system. The advantage of this is that whenever you need to give out any information about yourself it will be so much *easier* than at present – no completing forms, just transfer across the relevant bits. Or companies can access your system and pull off the relevant data, subject to your permission.

Are people becoming more willing to let their personal details be stored on network devices? What are the potential pitfalls here? The police should normally have access only to your criminal record, the doctor only to your medical notes, your various banks only to their own account details. Who will guarantee this restricted access? How will you be able to check that it is not being violated?

Government and censorship

Government, so far, has had little influence on the shape of interactive media. It had a hand at the birth of the Internet (which grew out of the older ARPANET system, funded by the

US military to link scientists at different institutions), but has since been conspicuously absent. Many Internet enthusiasts would like to keep government in all its guises – regulation, standard-setting, censorship and taxes – well away.

Networks and cheap telephone tariffs mean that more information-processing companies (and even individuals) may start to operate from countries with low direct taxes. Electronic commerce can also make it easier for shoppers to evade sales taxes, for example, by purchasing through offshore suppliers.

Censorship by government will be an issue, especially for those countries out of tune with the American way of life. What can a state do if it does not want its citizens reading material which its rulers deem profane or seditious? How will dictatorial governments react to information sites which criticize the ruling party? Even the US is not exempt from censorship: countries such as Holland and Sweden have more liberal laws on pornography.

Most crime on the Internet is covered by present laws, but these are invoked only when a company is caught. Checking the Web (globally) for any sites which contain illegal material is increasingly difficult. It is almost impossible if you are a small country, English is not the national language, and you have many laws which will be broken by US sites. Realistically for the foreseeable future, US rules will become world rules. The only practical way for a government or religious community to restrict what its citizens/members can access is by excluding everything that has not been specifically allowed.

In terms of which countries will be winners and losers in the digital revolution, the evidence suggests that the US and Scandinavia (which are already ahead) and South-East Asia (with its young population and dynamic economies) will all benefit, while most of Western Europe will generally suffer.

Voting and community involvement
The local information network may over time supersede the local newspaper, although a likely outcome is that the same

publisher will run both. The local newspaper is often free because it is supported by classified ads. As advertising migrates to a searchable medium, so local news and information will follow. Many people care more about their local community than about bigger and more remote issues (foreign policy, a unified monetary system), and so will take the effort to make their views known online if it is their local school which is being discussed in the council chamber. So the information network will not only provide the means whereby virtual communities seed and flourish, it may also help to cement the local physical community.

There is a view that the information network will involve us more in the democratic process. Yes and no. It may achieve little to ask the (online) public to vote electronically on policy matters, if only because the voting sample would be unbalanced by special interest groups. Also, it could encourage governments to opt out of difficult decisions by increasingly holding referenda on divisive issues. Even if online technology were universally available, the evidence is that the ability to vote electronically would not increase participation in national elections or referenda.

Looking further ahead

By some time in the second half of the twenty-first century, two developments are possible that raise serious philosophical, ethical and political questions. First, we may have technology that can 'read' or 'write' thoughts and feelings directly out of and into our brains. We accept that some of the processes of thinking and feeling can be 'read' – at least in crude terms – using modern brain scanners. But the idea of technology that can read or induce mental states accurately and reliably is not a comfortable one, raising serious issues of control.

Second, at some stage there will be computers more intelligent than people. The timing is hard to predict: the main result of artificial intelligence research to date has been to show that many of the skills we take for granted – like walking and talking – are much more complex than they seem. Even something as well structured as playing chess turned out to involve holistic processes like pattern recognition and feelings. Forty years ago, most experts thought it would take perhaps ten years for a computer to beat the best human chess player in the world. Although it took forty years, not ten, this has now happened. What will happen if, in another forty years, machines are finally more intelligent than people? Will they treat us as badly as we treat other animals?

And finally

Much discussion of future media is dominated by a kind of breathless enthusiasm. In this brief review, we have tried to be more balanced. Both the speed and many of the benefits of the digital revolution have been overhyped, and some of its dangers and disadvantages underplayed. Like genetic engineering, it will quite soon confront us with deep philosophical and ethical questions about the nature of humanity. The ultimate risk is that we, or our grandchildren, end up in a nightmare world dominated by machines.

The best protection against these dangers is a citizenry that is informed, involved, alert and questioning. We hope that *The Future of Media* will contribute to the development of such a citizenry. Of course, there are many other personal and professional reasons for finding out about, and experimenting with, digital media. Perhaps the most important is this: for most people in today's advanced economies, the digital revolution is likely to be the most interesting and wide-ranging social development of their lifetimes.

Some of you will find the scenarios we have described in this essay fanciful, others will feel that they are too cautious. We have aimed to predict realistically how media will influence home life in the next decade or so. Most, if not all, that we have described is happening now, somewhere.

Further Reading

To explore the issues in this book more fully, a good starting-point is *Being Digital* by Nicholas Negroponte (Knopf, 1995). Negroponte, Director of the Media Lab at MIT, saw the importance of media becoming digital long before most experts. He believes that the digital revolution will be radical, fast and mostly beneficial. The Media Lab focuses on making technology easy for people to communicate with.

The Road Ahead by Bill Gates, Chairman of software giant Microsoft (Viking, 1995), is part autobiography, partly a history of the computer industry, but mostly Gates's view of the likely impact of digital technology on entertainment, commerce, education and society.

Frances Cairncross is a senior editor at *The Economist*. Her wide-ranging *The Death of Distance* (Orion, 1997) reviews the convergence of the telephone, television and computer, and the implications of the collapsing cost of electronic communication, especially over long distances. Topics include the further globalization of business operations, the glut of information but scarcity of key content, the growing importance of both price competition and brands and the increasing difficulty of nation-state government.

Governance is further explored in *Release 2.0: A Design for Living in the Digital Age* by Esther Dyson (Broadway Books, 1997). Dyson's Release 1.0 newsletter and annual PC Forum are highly influential among the top US digerati. *Release 2.0* is about ensuring that the digital revolution makes the World more, not less, civilized, by intelligently addressing governance, content ownership and control, privacy, anonymity and security.

The One-to-One Future by Don Peppers and Martha Rogers

(Piatkus, 1993) is about the impact of digital technology on marketing. Peppers and Rogers argue that mass media and marketing will be replaced by interactive, individually customized media and marketing, 'building business relationships one customer at a time'. They also discuss privacy and other societal impacts.

Television and its Audience by Patrick Barwise, Andrew Ehrenberg, and Douglas Carrie (Sage, 2nd edition forthcoming) gives the background to the section on television in this book. It focuses mainly on the patterns of multichannel viewing behaviour, but also covers related issues such as TV advertising.

HAL's Legacy, edited by David G. Stork (MIT Press, 1997), is partly a tribute to Arthur C. Clarke's late-60s novel and Stanley Kubrick's movie *2001: A Space Odyssey*, and partly a review of the state-of-the-art and future prospects in artificial intelligence. The contributors include many of the top US researchers on computer science, voice processing, artificial intelligence, etc., but the writing is readable and mostly nontechnical.

The Media Equation by Byron Reeves and Clifford Nass (Cambridge University Press, 1996) is about 'how people treat computers, television and new media like real people and places'. For instance, Reeves and Nass's research at Stanford University shows that people are polite to computers, respond differently to male and female computer voices and feel threatened by a large face on a PC screen.

Kevin Warwick is Professor of Cybernetics at Reading University. His *March of the Machines: Why the New Race of Robots Will Rule the World* (Century, 1997) explores the frightening long-term implications of the continuing growth of machine intelligence. Today's robots can learn, communicate, teach each other and treat human beings as objects or resources in their environment. Tomorrow's will also be smarter than people.

Tips for Time Travellers by Peter Cochrane, Head of Research at BT (Orion, 1997) also discusses the radical implications of digital technology, but more optimistically than Kevin Warwick. It consists of sixty 600-word chapters, ranging from purely practical issues like network reliability and voice processing, to philosophical questions such as whether our minds could outlive us within a computer. Full of ideas about the manifold knock-on effects of new technology in the twenty-first century.